Children's
PICTURE
ATLAS

by Julia Adams

illustrated by Amelia Herbertson

ARCTURUS

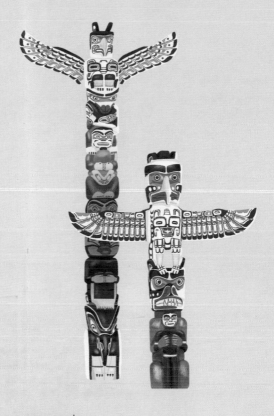

ARCTURUS

This edition published in 2022 by Arcturus Publishing Limited
26/27 Bickels Yard, 151–153 Bermondsey Street,
London SE1 3HA

Author: Julia Adams
Illustrator: Amelia Herbertson
Cartographer: Lovell Johns
Editor: Violet Peto
Designer: Linda Storey, Top Floor Design Ltd
Design Manager: Jessica Holliland
Managing Editor: Joe Harris

ISBN: 978-1-3988-1442-4
CH008273NT
Supplier 42, Date 0821, Print run 11696

Printed in Singapore

CONTENTS

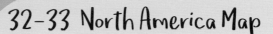

WELCOME TO OUR WORLD!

NORTH PACIFIC OCEAN

NORTH AMERICA

NORTH ATLANTIC OCEAN

Yellow areas on the map show hot deserts. These are habitats that are extremely hot during the day and have very little rainfall. The Sahara is the world's largest hot desert.

SAHARA

The world is divided up into landmasses called continents. Each continent is made up of different countries and habitats.

This map explains all the symbols and features used in this book.

SOUTH AMERICA

Around the world, huge tropical rain forests line the Equator. Here, the weather is warm and wet all year round. The Amazon is the largest rain forest on Earth.

SOUTH PACIFIC OCEAN

SOUTH ATLANTIC OCEAN

Mountain symbols with craters and lava tell us where major active volcanoes are in the world.

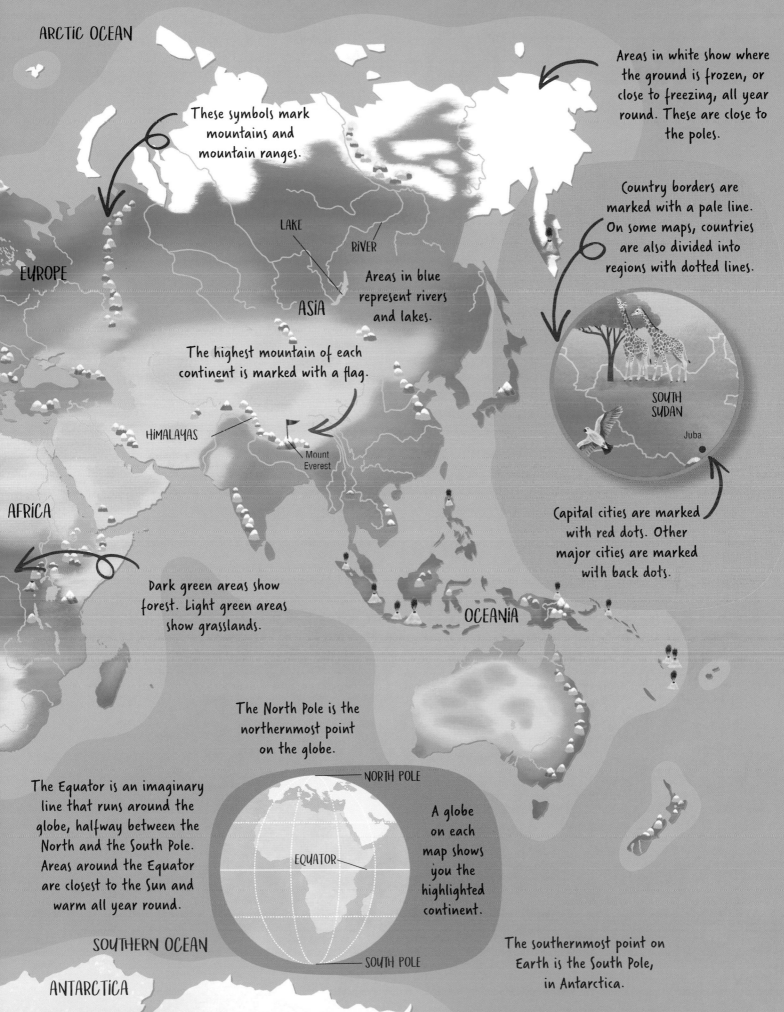

ARCTIC OCEAN

These symbols mark mountains and mountain ranges.

Areas in white show where the ground is frozen, or close to freezing, all year round. These are close to the poles.

EUROPE

LAKE

RIVER

Country borders are marked with a pale line. On some maps, countries are also divided into regions with dotted lines.

ASIA

Areas in blue represent rivers and lakes.

The highest mountain of each continent is marked with a flag.

HIMALAYAS

Mount Everest

SOUTH SUDAN

Juba

AFRICA

Capital cities are marked with red dots. Other major cities are marked with back dots.

Dark green areas show forest. Light green areas show grasslands.

OCEANIA

The North Pole is the northernmost point on the globe.

The Equator is an imaginary line that runs around the globe, halfway between the North and the South Pole. Areas around the Equator are closest to the Sun and warm all year round.

NORTH POLE

A globe on each map shows you the highlighted continent.

EQUATOR

SOUTHERN OCEAN

SOUTH POLE

ANTARCTICA

The southernmost point on Earth is the South Pole, in Antarctica.

5

AFRICA

Welcome to the world's second-largest continent! Africa's landscapes range from snowy mountains and lush rain forests to hot deserts and vast grasslands. Surrounding the continent, coral reefs and kelp forests are home to turtles, sharks, fish, and many other ocean creatures.

WHERE WE ARE FROM

The Great Rift Valley, which stretches across Djibouti, Eritrea, Ethiopia, Sudan, Uganda, Kenya, and Tanzania, is the place where scientists believe we first evolved. Ancient cave paintings tell us about the life of our ancestors.

POPULATION: 1.3 billion
NUMBER OF COUNTRIES: 54
HOTTEST PLACE: Al-ʻAzīzīyah (Libya), 58°C (136°F)
COLDEST PLACE: Ifrane (Morocco), -24°C (-11°F)
HIGHEST MOUNTAIN: Kilimanjaro (Tanzania), 5,895 m (19,340 ft)

RECORD-BREAKING HEAT

Africa is the hottest continent on Earth. The Sahara, which covers most of northern Africa, is the world's largest hot desert. Here, temperatures can reach over 50°C (122°F).

AZORES (PORTUGAL)

MADEIRA (PORTUGAL)

CANARY ISLANDS (SPAIN)

Laayoune

WESTERN SAHARA

MAURITANIA

CAPE VERDE   Nouakchott

SENEGAL

Praia   Dakar

Banjul

THE GAMBIA

Bissau

GUINEA-BISSAU   GUINEA

Conakry   SIERRA
Freetown   LEONE

Monrovia

LIBERIA

Find out more about the Egyptian pyramids on page 9.

At 6,650 km (4,130 mi), the Nile is the longest river on Earth!

Great Rift Valley

The towering Sossusvlei sand dunes of the Namib desert are up to 400 m (1,312 ft) high!

Wild ring-tailed lemurs only live on the island of Madagascar.

MOROCCO
abat
Algiers
Tunis
TUNISIA
Tripoli
ALGERIA
LIBYA
EGYPT
Cairo
MALI
NIGER
CHAD
SUDAN
Khartoum
ERITREA
Asmara
DJIBOUTI
Djibouti
BURKINA FASO
Niamey
NIGERIA
N'Djamena
Ouagadougou
Abuja
Addis Ababa
BENIN
TOGO
IVORY COAST
GHANA
Lagos
CENTRAL AFRICAN REPUBLIC
SOUTH SUDAN
ETHIOPIA
SOMALIA
Yamoussoukro
Lomé
Porto-Novo
Accra
CAMEROON
Bangui
Juba
Mogadishu
Malabo
Yaoundé
EQUATORIAL GUINEA
São Tomé
GABON
CONGO
UGANDA
Kampala
KENYA
SEYCHELLES
SÃO TOMÉ AND PRÍNCIPE
Libreville
DEMOCRATIC REPUBLIC OF CONGO
RWANDA
Kigali
Nairobi
Victoria
Brazzaville
BURUNDI
Bujumbura
Kinshasa
Luanda
Dodoma
TANZANIA
INDIAN OCEAN
Moroni
ATLANTIC OCEAN
ANGOLA
ZAMBIA
MALAWI
COMOROS
MADAGASCAR
Lusaka
Lilongwe
MOZAMBIQUE
Antananarivo
MAURITIUS
Port Louis
NAMIBIA
ZIMBABWE
Harare
RÉUNION (FRANCE)
Windhoek
BOTSWANA
Gaborone
Pretoria
Mbabane
Maputo
Lobamba
ESWATINI
Bloemfontein
Maseru
SOUTH AFRICA
LESOTHO
Cape Town

AFRICAN ANIMALS

Despite their name, many eastern lowland gorillas live high up in the mountains. The males are called "silverbacks" because of the silvery fur on their backs and hips.

These apes live in families, just like us!

Chimpanzees are our closest relatives. They can walk on their hind legs and use tools to find food.

Lions live in groups, or prides, of up to 40 animals. The females are extremely good hunters.

Lions are the only cats with a tail tassel.

AFRICAN MONUMENTS

The pyramids of Giza, in Egypt, were built over 4,500 years ago for the ancient pharaohs. Close by is the Great Sphinx—a huge statue with a human head and a lion's body.

It took up to 20 years to build each pyramid!

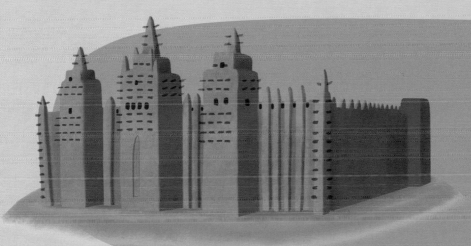

The Great Mosque of Djenné, in Mali, is the largest building in the world to be made of earth and sand. It is over 100 years old.

The Laas Geel cave paintings can be found in Somalia, in the Great Rift Valley. They are some of the oldest artworks on Earth, made about 20,000 years ago.

The rock art includes a painting of a pet dog!

AFRICAN CITIES

Lagos, the largest city in Nigeria, has a population of over 20 million. It stretches out across an area called the mainland, as well as many islands, and is home to one of Africa's busiest ports.

Lagos has a mix of interesting buildings, including the National Arts Theatre.

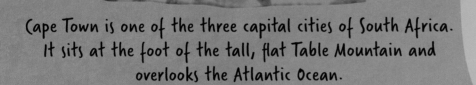

Cape Town is one of the three capital cities of South Africa. It sits at the foot of the tall, flat Table Mountain and overlooks the Atlantic Ocean.

Table Mountain has a level plateau about 3 km (1.86 mi) from side to side.

Port Louis is the capital city of the island state of Mauritius, far out in the Indian Ocean. It is home to many different cultures and religions. The historical Jummah Mosque was built here in 1852.

AFRICAN NATURE

The Maasai Mara is a Kenyan nature reserve that stretches across huge, grassy plains. Every year, millions of gazelles, zebras, and wildebeest migrate here to escape the dry period further south.

Victoria Falls is the largest waterfall in the world, at 1,708 m (5,604 ft) long and 108 m (345 ft) high. Its local name is Mosi-oa-Tunya, which means "smoke that thunders."

Hot springs, acid pools, and a bubbling, red lake make up the incredible landscape of Ethiopia's Danakil Depression. It is one of the hottest, driest, and lowest places on Earth.

The lava lake in the Danakil Depression is one of only six in the world!

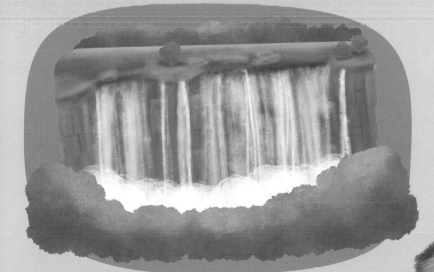

As the spray of the waterfall catches the sunlight, it forms constant rainbows.

EUROPE

Although Europe is the second-smallest continent, it covers many different landscapes. From towering mountains and snow-covered forests to grassy plains and even desert-like areas, this continent has many different environments!

SUNNY SOUTH, ICY NORTH

In the south of Europe lies the Mediterranean region. Here, summers are long and hot, perfect for growing citrus fruits, grapes, and olives. The northern area of the continent is part of the Arctic. Lakes and seas freeze over in winter, and temperatures can plunge to -50°C (-58 °F).

POPULATION: 750 million
NUMBER OF COUNTRIES: 46
HOTTEST PLACE: Seville (Spain), 50°C (122°F)
COLDEST PLACE: Ust' Shchugor (Russia), -55°C (-67°F)
HIGHEST MOUNTAIN: Mount Elbrus (Russia), 5,642 m (18,510 ft)

SIMMERING HEAT

Although Europe doesn't have as many volcanoes as some continents, it does have one of the world's most active ones. Mount Etna on the Italian island of Sicily stands 3,263 m (10,705 ft) tall. In between regular eruptions, a steady plume of smoke rises out of its craters.

	Capital		Country	Capital
1	Amsterdam	A	LIECHTENSTEIN	Vaduz
2	Brussels	B	MONACO	Monaco
3	Luxembourg	C	SAN MARINO	San Marino
4	Bcrnc	D	SLOVENIA	Ljubljana
5	Zagreb	E	BOSNIA AND HERZEGOVINA	Sarajevo
6	Tirana	F	MONTENEGRO	Podgorica
7	Skopje	G	MOLDOVA	Chisinau

ARCTIC OCEAN

In the winter, the Arctic fox grows a white coat to blend in with the snow and ice.

The balalaika is a traditional Russian stringed instrument.

ATLANTIC OCEAN

ICELAND
Reykjavik

NORWAY
SWEDEN
FINLAND
Helsinki
Oslo
Stockholm
Tallinn
ESTONIA
LATVIA
Riga
LITHUANIA
Vilnius
RUSSIA
Moscow

DENMARK
Copenhagen

UNITED KINGDOM
Dublin
IRELAND
London
NETHERLANDS
1
Berlin
GERMANY
POLAND
Warsaw
Minsk
BELARUS
Kiev
UKRAINE

Stonehenge is an ancient monument made up of huge, standing rocks.

2 BELGIUM
3 LUXEMBOURG
Paris
Prague
CZECH REPUBLIC
Vienna
AUSTRIA
SLOVAKIA
Budapest
HUNGARY

The Winter Palace used to be home to the Czar, the ruler of the Russian Empire.

4 A
SWITZERLAND
FRANCE
D 5
CROATIA
ROMANIA
Belgrade
Bucharest
G

ANDORRA
Andorra La Vella
CORSICA (FRANCE)
B
C
ITALY
Rome
E
F
SERBIA
KOSOVO
6 7
BULGARIA
Sofia

PORTUGAL
Lisbon
Madrid
SPAIN
SARDINIA (ITALY)
ALBANIA
NORTH MACEDONIA
GREECE
Athens
TURKEY

Borscht is a traditional eastern European soup.

SICILY (ITALY)
Valletta
MALTA
CRETE (GREECE)

13

EUROPEAN ANIMALS

European bison used to live all across Europe. Today, they are only at home in the ancient Białowieża Forest in Poland.

Flamingoes are pink because of the algae they eat.

When winter comes to their African home, flamingoes migrate to southern Spain. Here, they breed and raise their young before it's time to return south.

Puffins nest high up on the cliffs of the Faroe Islands. They dive into the ocean to catch small fish with their bright, specially shaped beaks.

EUROPEAN MONUMENTS

Built by the ancient Romans, the Colosseum, in Italy, was used as a venue for gladiator fights and shows.

The megalithic temples of Malta are some of the oldest freestanding stone structures in the world. They were built 5,500 years ago.

The Parthenon is an ancient temple that was built 2,500 years ago. It stands on the Acropolis, a hill high above Greece's capital city, Athens.

The Parthenon used to be brightly painted.

EUROPEAN CITIES

Berlin, Germany, was once divided by a wall into east and west, while Germany was split into two countries. Since 1990, the country is one again, with Berlin as its capital.

The Brandenburg Gate is a symbol of togetherness.

Istanbul, Turkey, is the largest city in Europe, with over 15 million people. The Mosque of Hagia Sofia is one of its most famous landmarks.

Istanbul sits on two continents —Europe and Asia.

Moscow, Russia's capital, is the largest city in the country. One of its most important buildings is St. Basil's Cathedral.

EUROPEAN NATURE

The lakes, waterfalls, and caves of Plitvice Lakes National Park in Croatia have formed over thousands of years. Its forests are home to wolves, bears, and many kinds of birds.

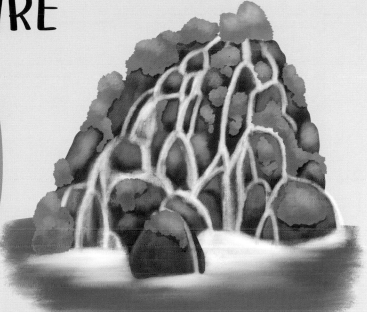

Over 300 kinds of butterflies live in this national park!

Iceland is famous for its many geysers. Geysers are hot springs that suddenly shoot boiling hot water and steam high up into the air.

 Geysers can reach a height of 170 m (558 ft)!

The Camargue in southern France is an area of marshes, swamps, and bright pink salt lakes. It is also home to semi-wild horses and flamingoes.

ASIA

Stretching from the Arabian Peninsula in the west to the Pacific Ocean in the east, and from the Arctic Russian north to the tropical islands of Indonesia in the south, Asia is the biggest continent in the world.

Country	Capital
Ⓐ CYPRUS	Nicosia
Ⓑ LEBANON	Beirut
Ⓒ SYRIA	Damascus
Ⓓ ISRAEL	Jerusalem
Ⓔ JORDAN	Amman
Ⓕ ARMENIA	Yerevan
Ⓖ GEORGIA	Tbilisi
Ⓗ AZERBAIJAN	Baku
Ⓘ KUWAIT	Kuwait City
Ⓙ BAHRAIN	Manama
Ⓚ QATAR	Doha
Ⓛ UNITED ARAB EMIRATES	Abu Dhabi
Ⓜ MALDIVES	Malé
Ⓝ BHUTAN	Thimphu
Ⓞ SINGAPORE	Singapore
Ⓟ BRUNEI	Bandar Seri Begawan
Ⓠ TIMOR-LESTE	Dili

A CONTINENT OF EXTREMES

Asia is both home to the highest mountain in the world—Mount Everest—and the lowest place in the world—the coast of the Dead Sea. Siberia, in Russia, is one of the coldest places on Earth outside of Antarctica, while the Arabian Desert is one of the hottest!

TURKEY

Ankara

A
B
D
E

HOME TO MANY

Over 4 billion people live in Asia—more than on all other continents put together. Cities such as Shanghai in China and Karachi in Pakistan have over 20 million residents. Even so, there are large areas where hardly anyone lives, like Siberia in Russia and the Plateau of Tibet in China.

POPULATION: 4.6 billion
NUMBER OF COUNTRIES: 49
HOTTEST PLACE: Tirat Tsvi (Israel), 54°C (129°F)
COLDEST PLACE: Verkhoyansk (Russia), −68°C (−90°F)
HIGHEST MOUNTAIN: Mount Everest (Nepal/China), 8,848 m / 19,029 ft

The Trans-Siberian Express runs on the longest railroad in the world, covering 9,300 km (5,780 mi).

The king eider is an Arctic sea duck, famous for its thick, soft plumage.

Lena Pillars Nature Park in Siberia, Russia is named after the towering stone pillars that have formed along Lena River.

RUSSIA

PACIFIC OCEAN

Nur-Sultan

KAZAKHSTAN

Ulaanbaatar

MONGOLIA

F

G

UZBEKISTAN

Bishek

H

TURKMENISTAN

Tashkent

KYRGYZSTAN

Beijing

NORTH KOREA
Pyongyang

Ashgabat

TAJIKISTAN

CHINA

Sejong
Seoul

JAPAN

Tokyo

Tehran

Kabul

Islamabad

SOUTH KOREA

Baghdad

IRAN

AFGHANISTAN

IRAQ

I

PAKISTAN

New
Delhi

NEPAL

Kathmandu

N

J

K

MYANMAR

Riyadh

L

BANGLADESH

Muscat

Dhaka

Nay Pyi
Taw

SAUDI
ARABIA

INDIA

OMAN

Vientiane

Hanoi

YEMEN

THAILAND

LAOS

Manila

PHILIPPINES

Sana'a

Bangkok

CAMBODIA

VIETNAM

Sri Jayawardenepura Kotte

SRI LANKA

Phnom
Penh

Colombo

MALAYSIA

P

M

INDIAN OCEAN

Kuala Lumpur
Putrajaya

O

Jakarta

INDONESIA

Q

ASIAN ANIMALS

High up in the snowy mountains, Japanese macaques keep warm in the winter by bathing in the local hot springs.

These macaques are often called snow monkeys.

Giant pandas are some of the rarest animals on Earth. They only feed on bamboo and live in mountainous forests in central China.

Panda mothers are 800 times heavier than their newborns!

The Bengal tiger is at home in the vast wetlands of the Bay of Bengal. It is one of the world's largest big cats and can hunt prey that is larger than itself.

ASIAN MONUMENTS

The Great Wall of China was built over 2,000 years ago, to protect the ancient Chinese empire from its enemies.

All in all, the Great Wall is 21,196 km (13,170 mi) long.

The Kaaba is a structure in Mecca, Saudi Arabia. It is the most holy site in Islam, and the direction in which Muslims around the world pray.

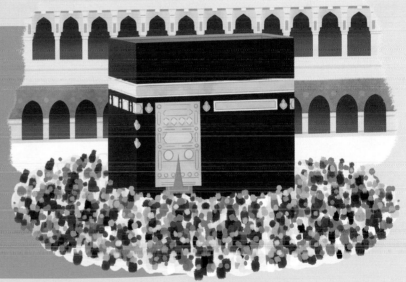

The walled city of Hué used to be Vietnam's capital. It has many monuments, gardens, temples, and royal buildings.

The walls protecting the city are 2 m (6.5 ft) thick.

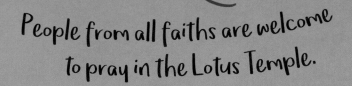

People from all faiths are welcome to pray in the Lotus Temple.

New Delhi, the Indian capital, is one of the largest cities in the world. Its Lotus Temple, which looks like a flower, is one of the most visited places on Earth.

Seoul, South Korea, is one of the fastest-growing cities. Traditional temples and palaces and modern, towering skyscrapers stand side-by-side.

Tehran, Iran's capital, is one of the highest cities on Earth. Milad Tower looks out over the bustling city and the nearby Alborz Mountains.

The Lotte Tower is South Korea's tallest building at 555 m (1,820 ft).

Dubai is perched between the Persian Gulf and the Arabian Desert. The capital city of the United Arab Emirates is known for the Burj Khalifa—the world's tallest building.

Dubai's nickname is the City of Gold.

Hong Kong is the city with the most skyscrapers in the world. It is densely packed, with a lot of people living in a relatively small area.

The top of Marina Bay Sands is shaped like a ship.

Singapore is a city state, which means that it is a city that is its own country. Its most famous building, the Marina Bay Sands, overlooks the city's busy coast.

ASIAN NATURE

The taiga is a thick pine and spruce forest which stretches across Russia, south of the Arctic. Wolves, bears, and Ural owls are some of the animals that live here.

In parts of the Russian taiga, winter can last nine months.

The Plateau of Tibet is a large area of land that is high up in the Himalayan Mountains. Snow leopards, yaks, and red pandas live in this remote area.

Borneo is Asia's largest island. Its lush rain forest is home to orangutans, dragon lizards, and the rafflesia flower, which measures 1 m (3 ft) across!

The Plateau of Tibet is often called the Roof of the World.

The ground of the tundra along Russia's north coast is frozen all year round. Despite this, animals such as musk oxen, Arctic hares, and Arctic terns live here.

The tundra is too cold for trees to grow.

The Caspian Sea's waves are home to the Caspian seal and the huge beluga sturgeon, which can grow longer than 5 m (16 ft). Spur-thighed tortoises graze on the sea's shores.

While temperatures in the Gobi Desert reach 45°C (113°F) in the summer, they plunge to an icy −40°C (−40°F) in the winter.

Bactrian camels, Przewalski's horses, and bearded vultures thrive in these extreme temperatures.

OCEANIA

Stretched across the south Pacific Ocean, Oceania covers Australia, New Zealand, and about 10,000 islands both large and small. While this continent doesn't experience extreme cold, there are a lot of intensely hot and dry places, especially in the heart of Australia.

Male birds of paradise have bright feathers to attract females.

NORTHERN MARIANA ISLANDS (USA)
- Saipan

GUAM (USA)

FEDERATED STATES OF MICRONESIA
- Palikir

PALAU
- Ngerulmud

PAPUA NEW GUINEA
- Port Moresby

SOLOMON ISLANDS
- Honiara

Darwin

NORTHERN TERRITORY

AUSTRALIA

WESTERN AUSTRALIA

QUEENSLAND

SOUTH AUSTRALIA

- Brisbane

NEW SOUTH WALES

Perth •

Adelaide •

- Sydney

Canberra •

VICTORIA

Melbourne •

TAZMANIA

• Hobart

THE FIRST SETTLERS

Australia's Aboriginal people settled here over 65,000 years ago. In the 1700s, Europeans arrived. They colonized and took land. Today, the culture is mostly European, but indigenous rights and history are more protected.

The inner yellow and orange part of the hala fruit is sweet and tastes a bit like mango.

MARSHALL ISLANDS
Majuro

HAWAII (USA)

Surfing has been part of Hawaiian culture for over 1,000 years.

Many of Oceania's islands are part of the Pacific Ring of Fire, an area in the Pacific Ocean that has many active volcanoes and strong earthquakes.

NAURU (no capital city)
Yaren

South Tarawa
KIRIBATI

TUVALU
Funafuti

TOKELAU (NZ)

COOK ISLANDS (NZ)

WALLIS AND FUTUNA (FRANCE)
Mata-Utu
Apia
SAMOA

AMERICAN SAMOA (USA)

VANUATU
Port Vila

Suva
FIJI

NIUE (NZ)

The slit drum is often played during an "ura," or drum dance.

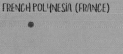

FRENCH POLYNESIA (FRANCE)

Nouméa

TONGA
Nuku'alofa

NEW CALEDONIA (FRANCE)

PACIFIC OCEAN

PITCAIRN ISLANDS (UK)

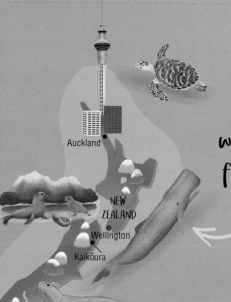

Kaikoura's coast is one of the only spots on Earth where sperm whales feed all year round.

Auckland

NEW ZEALAND
Wellington
Kaikoura

POPULATION: 39.7 million
NUMBER OF COUNTRIES: 14
HOTTEST PLACE: Oodnadatta (Australia), 50.7°C (123.3°F)
COLDEST PLACE: Ranfurly (New Zealand), -14.1°C (-6.6°F)
HIGHEST MOUNTAIN: Mount Wilhelm (Papua New Guinea), 4,509 m (14,793 ft)

27

OCEANIA ANIMALS

Red kangaroos are the largest kind of kangaroo. They can cover 8 m (26 ft) in one leap, and reach speeds of more than 55 km/h (35 mph).

Baby red kangaroos, or joeys, shelter in their mother's pouch for about seven months.

With their powerful legs and strong claws, coconut crabs can easily scale tall palm trees and crack open coconuts. This has earned them the nickname "coconut thief!"

Tuataras can live to be 100 years old!

Tuataras only live in New Zealand. Their name comes from the Māori language and means "peaks on the back." They are related to reptiles that lived during the dinosaur age.

OCEANIA MONUMENTS

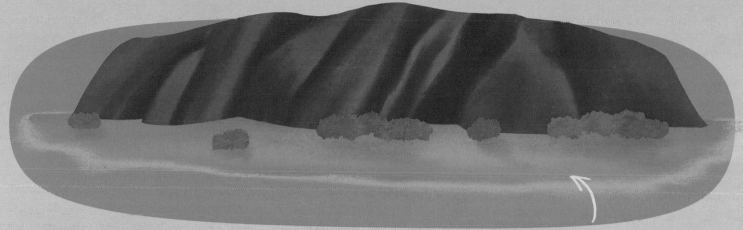

Uluru is a tall, wide mountain of red rock that stands on Aboriginal land. It has been an important and sacred structure to the Anangu people for tens of thousands of years.

Ancient Anangu rock art on Uluru often tells traditional stories.

The people of Lelu used a lot of coral from the sea to build their city.

The Lelu ruins are the remains of a large walled city that was built over 700 years ago. It had tall walls, a system of canals, and paved roads.

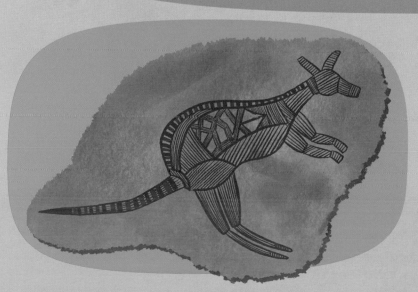

The rock art in Kakadu National Park, Australia, is over 20,000 years old. It tells us about the history of the Bininj and Mungguy people, and what life was like in ancient Australia.

OCEANIA CITIES

Sydney, Australia, has over 5.4 million people, making it the largest city in Oceania. Aboriginal people have lived in the area for over 30,000 years, while modern Sydney was founded in 1788.

It took about seven years to engineer and build the roof of the Sydney Opera House.

Auckland, or Tāmaki Makaurau, is New Zealand's largest city. It is overlooked by the Sky Tower, which stands at 328 m (1,076 ft) and is the tallest structure in the southern hemisphere.

Port Moresby, Papua New Guinea, was named by a British captain and founded in 1888. However, the Koitabu and Motu people have lived in traditional stilt houses around the area for over 1,000 years.

The National Parliament building is decorated with traditional paintings.

OCEANIA NATURE

The corals of the Great Barrier Reef form an underwater structure that is about the size of Japan. It is home to over 4,500 different species of ocean animal.

Coral is built by tiny creatures, called polyps, over hundreds of years.

Hawaii National Park surrounds Kīlauea and Mauna Loa, two of the world's most active volcanoes. The 'i'iwi, Hawaiian hoary bat, and kamehameha butterfly live here.

The kea is the only mountain parrot in the world. It lives by Aoraki/Mount Cook.

Te Wahipounamu is a huge nature park which covers most of south-west New Zealand. It is home to the powelliphanta, a meat-eating snail, and the New Zealand fur seal, or kekeno.

NORTH AMERICA

North America is the third-largest continent in the world. Stretching from the Pacific Ocean in the west to the Atlantic Ocean in the east, and from the Arctic north to the tropical south, it has many different kinds of landscapes and climates.

SETTLER STATES

For thousands of years, North America has been home to many different indigenous communities. From the 1500s, European settlers arrived, taking a lot of indigenous homeland and introducing new traditions and languages. To this day, many indigenous people live in their communities and keep their culture alive.

POPULATION: 580 million
NUMBER OF COUNTRIES: 23
HOTTEST PLACE: Death Valley (USA), 57°C (135°F)
COLDEST PLACE: Klinck research station (Greenland), −69°C (−92°F)
HIGHEST MOUNTAIN: Denali (USA), 6,194 m (20,321 ft)

49

YUKON

BRITISH
COLUMB

PACIFIC
OCEAN

1

14

25

The Bighorn medicine wheel is a sacred site for Native Americans. It is close to 1,000 years old.

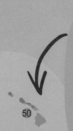

50

Hawaii is a US state that geographically belongs to Oceania (see page 27).

Ice fishers camp on frozen lakes and drill holes in the ice to catch fish.

States of the USA

1	WASHINGTON	11	VERMONT	21	INDIANA	31	KENTUCKY	41	LOUISIANA
2	MONTANA	12	NEW HAMPSHIRE	22	OHIO	32	WEST VIRGINIA	42	MISSISSIPPI
3	NORTH DAKOTA	13	MAINE	23	PENNSYLVANIA	33	VIRGINIA	43	TENNESSEE
4	MINNESOTA	14	OREGON	24	NEW JERSEY	34	MARYLAND	44	ALABAMA
5	WISCONSIN	15	IDAHO	25	CALIFORNIA	35	DELAWARE	45	FLORIDA
6	MICHIGAN	16	WYOMING	26	NEVADA	36	ARIZONA	46	GEORGIA
7	NEW YORK	17	SOUTH DAKOTA	27	UTAH	37	NEW MEXICO	47	SOUTH CAROLINA
8	CONNECTICUT	18	NEBRASKA	28	COLORADO	38	TEXAS	48	NORTH CAROLINA
9	RHODE ISLAND	19	IOWA	29	KANSAS	39	OKLAHOMA	49	ALASKA
10	MASSACHUSETTS	20	ILLINOIS	30	MISSOURI	40	ARKANSAS	50	HAWAII

GREENLAND (DENMARK)

NORTHWEST TERRITORIES

NUNAVUT

ALBERTA

CANADA

SASKATCHEWAN

MANITOBA

ONTARIO

QUEBEC

NEWFOUNDLAND AND LABRADOR

PRINCE EDWARD ISLAND

Ottawa

NOVA SCOTIA

NEW BRUNSWICK

Washington, D.C.

UNITED STATES OF AMERICA

MEXICO

ATLANTIC OCEAN

	Country	Capital
A	GUATEMALA	Guatemala City
B	EL SALVADOR	San Salvador
C	HONDURAS	Tegucigalpa
D	NICARAGUA	Managua
E	COSTA RICA	San José
F	PANAMA	Panama City
G	GRENADA	St George's
H	ST KITTS AND NEVIS	Basseterre
I	ANTIGUA AND BARBUDA	St John's
J	DOMINICA	Roseau
K	ST LUCIA	Castries
L	BARBADOS	Bridgetown
M	ST VINCENT AND THE GRENADINES	Kingstown
N	TRINIDAD AND TOBAGO	Port of Spain

Nassau

Havana

THE BAHAMAS

CUBA

Port-au-Prince

DOMINICAN REPUBLIC

Santo Domingo

JAMAICA

Mexico City

BELIZE

Belmopan

Kingston

HAITI

33

NORTH AMERICAN ANIMALS

Polar bears are excellent swimmers. They plunge into the icy Arctic waters to reach sea ice, where they hunt for ringed seals and other prey.

Underneath their white fur, polar bears have black skin!

The big, sturdy bison often lives in herds, grazing all year round. In the winter, it grows thick fur to protect itself from icy temperatures.

The bison is North America's largest land animal.

Every year, in October, hundreds of thousands of monarch butterflies migrate 4,000 km (2,485 mi) from southern Canada to Mexico to spend the winter.

NORTH AMERICAN MONUMENTS

Chichen Itza is an ancient Mayan city that was built over 1,000 years ago in modern-day Mexico. Its pyramid-shaped El Castillo temple has 365 steps leading to the top—one for each day of the year.

The Maya peoples have lived in and around Mexico for over 4,000 years.

The Native American community of Taos Pueblo has lived in the same village for over 1,000 years. They still live in the original houses, called adobe structures.

Petroglyphs Provincial Park, in Canada, is the site of over 900 ancient indigenous stone carvings, showing turtles and snakes, as well as humans.

Anishinaabe people call this sacred site Kinoomaagewaapkong—"the stones that teach."

NORTH AMERICAN CITIES

Vancouver's Stanley Park has a display of totem poles by indigenous artists.

Vancouver, in Canada, overlooks the Pacific Ocean and the Rocky Mountains.

It was founded in the 1870s by European colonizers.

New York City is the largest city in the USA, with over 8.5 million people. Its Statue of Liberty, on Liberty Island, welcomes visitors approaching from the Atlantic Ocean.

Mexico City was founded in 1325 by the Mexica people, the rulers of the Aztec empire. It is North America's oldest capital city.

The mosaic on the University of Mexico's library is the largest in the world.

NORTH AMERICAN NATURE

The thick, lush rain forest of Central America is home to hundreds of different kinds of birds, such as the eye-catching toucan.

Sloths and ocelots are excellent tree climbers.

The Everglades is the largest tropical wetland on Earth. During the wet season, a slow-moving river that is 97 km (60 miles) wide flows through the habitat.

Alligators, spoonbills, and marsh rabbits are at home in this swampy landscape.

In the heart of the Canadian Rocky Mountains lies Banff, the country's oldest national park. Grizzly bears, cougars, and bighorn sheep roam this protected area.

SOUTH AMERICA

Most of South America lies in the southern hemisphere. The Andes mountains run like a spine down the western coast of the continent. While hot, humid rain forests stretch across most of the northern half of the landmass, the far south is covered in ice and thick glaciers.

EXTREME HABITATS

The Atacama Desert along the coast of Chile and Peru is one of the driest areas in the world. Any water that reaches this desert comes from fog, drifting in from the Pacific Ocean. Meanwhile, in the north, the Colombian rain forest is one of the wettest places on Earth. Over 12,890 mm (507 in) of rain can fall here in a year.

Equator

POPULATION: 410 million
NUMBER OF COUNTRIES: 12
HOTTEST PLACE: Rivadavia (Argentina), 49°C (120°F)
COLDEST PLACE: Sarmiento (Argentina), -33°C (-27°F)
HIGHEST MOUNTAIN: Cerro Aconcagua (Argentina), 6,959 m (22,831 ft)

ANCIENT HISTORY

From the highest mountains to the thickest rain forests, South America has been home to indigenous peoples for thousands of years. From the 1500s, settlers from Spain and Portugal started colonizing the continent, splitting it into countries and taking land. Europeans called the Americas the "new world," although they have some of the oldest settlements in human history.

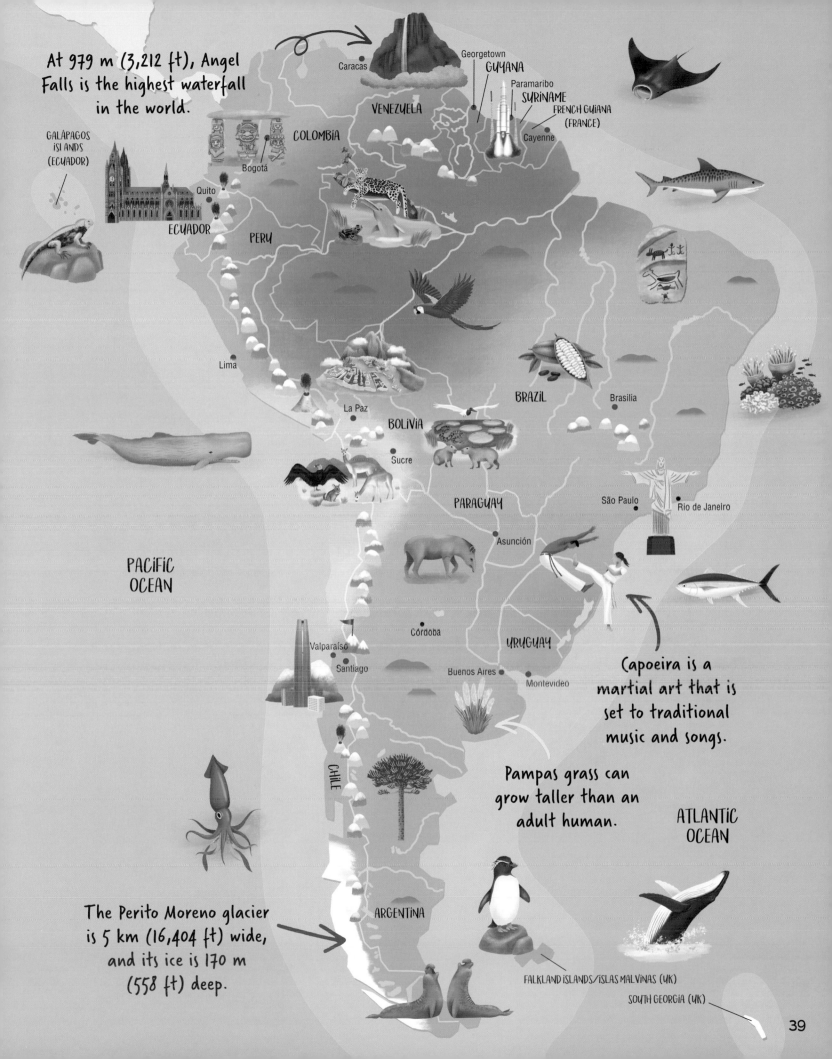

At 979 m (3,212 ft), Angel Falls is the highest waterfall in the world.

GALÁPAGOS ISLANDS (ECUADOR)

Caracas

Georgetown
GUYANA

Paramaribo
SURINAME
FRENCH GUIANA (FRANCE)

Cayenne

VENEZUELA

COLOMBIA

Bogotá

Quito

ECUADOR

PERU

Lima

La Paz

BOLIVIA

Sucre

BRAZIL

Brasilia

São Paulo

Rio de Janeiro

PARAGUAY

Asunción

PACIFIC OCEAN

Córdoba

URUGUAY

Valparaíso

Santiago

Buenos Aires

Montevideo

Capoeira is a martial art that is set to traditional music and songs.

Pampas grass can grow taller than an adult human.

ATLANTIC OCEAN

CHILE

ARGENTINA

The Perito Moreno glacier is 5 km (16,404 ft) wide, and its ice is 170 m (558 ft) deep.

FALKLAND ISLANDS/ISLAS MALVINAS (UK)

SOUTH GEORGIA (UK)

SOUTH AMERICAN ANIMALS

Tapirs are at home in the water as much as they are on land. They walk along riverbeds in the Amazon rain forest to find the plants they like eating.

When they are being attacked, tapirs dive underwater to shake off predators.

Marine iguanas only live on the shores of the Galápagos Islands. They dive into the cold ocean to graze on algae, then rest on rocks in the Sun to warm up again.

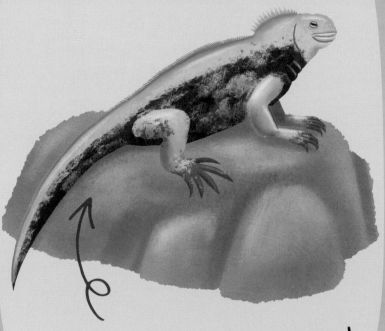

The marine iguana is the only lizard that spends time in the ocean!

Male southern elephant seals are the largest seals in the world. They weigh up to 4,000 kg (8,800 lb), which is six times more than a polar bear!

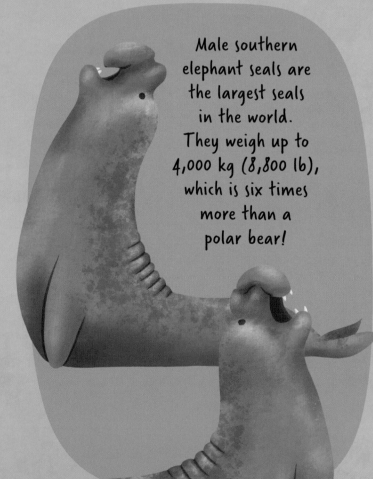

SOUTH AMERICAN MONUMENTS

Serra da Capivara National Park's rock art, in Brazil, is over 25,000 years old. It tells us about some of the first human communities in South America.

The paintings include animals, hunts, and scenes from everyday life.

Machu Picchu, an ancient Incan city, was built 600 years ago, high up in the Andes mountains in Peru. Today, its remains are popular with tourists from around the world.

San Agustín Archaeological Park, Colombia, is the largest ancient burial site in the world. Over 300 stone statues of animals and gods were carved more than 2,000 years ago to stand guard over the dead.

Some of the stone statues are over 4 m (13 ft) tall.

SOUTH AMERICAN CITIES

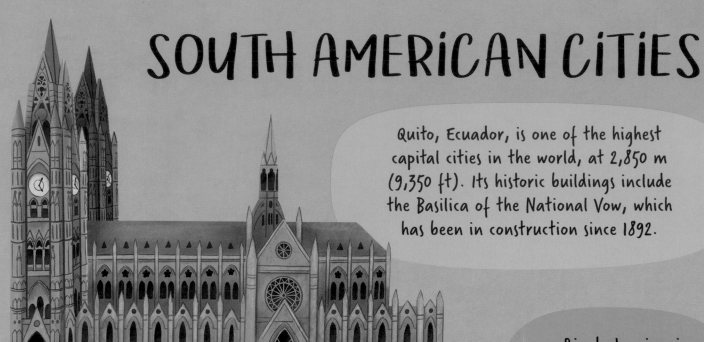

Quito, Ecuador, is one of the highest capital cities in the world, at 2,850 m (9,350 ft). Its historic buildings include the Basilica of the National Vow, which has been in construction since 1892.

Rio de Janeiro, in Brazil, sits on the Atlantic coast. It is home to the world's largest carnival, which is celebrated with huge parades across the city.

Santiago, Chile's capital, is a thriving city with views of the majestic Andes mountains.

The Christ the Redeemer statue overlooks Rio de Janeiro from Mount Corcovado.

The Gran Torre Santiago, Santiago's tallest building, is 300 m (984 ft) tall.

SOUTH AMERICAN NATURE

The Amazon river winds its way through the largest rain forest in the world. Many of the animals who live here aren't found anywhere else on Earth.

Amazon river dolphins, jaguars, and poison dart frogs live in the heart of the rain forest.

The Andes are the longest mountain range in the world, with some of the highest peaks in the Americas. The condor often builds its nests on these peaks, at heights of 5,000 m (16,000 ft).

The Pantanal wetlands are home to many unusual creatures and plants. Giant water lilies that can support the weight of a small child thrive alongside capybaras, anacondas, and jabirus.

Chinchillas and vicuñas have thick fur and wool to keep them warm in the freezing winters.

ANTARCTICA

The driest and coldest continent on Earth is Antarctica. It is covered in a thick sheet of ice, with winds that whip across it at speeds of up to 320 km/h (200 mph). Although many animals are at home here, humans only come for months at a time.

Nations from around the world have research stations on the icy landmass. Teams of scientists study the landscape, climate, and wildlife.

NEUMAYER (GERMANY)

Brunt Ice Shelf

CAPITÁN ARTURO PRAT (CHILE)

ESPERANZA (ARGENTINA)

HALLEY VI (UK)

Larsen B Ice Shelf

BELGRANO II (ARGENTINA)

ROTHERA (UK)

Filchner Ice Shelf

Ronne Ice Shelf

POLAR SEASONS

At Earth's poles, the year is divided into two seasons: summer and winter. The Antarctic winter lasts from March to September. During this time, the Sun never rises, and the ocean surrounding the continent is covered in thick ice. In October, the Sun rises and doesn't set again until March. The sea ice melts and many animals arrive to feed and have their young.

SOUTHERN OCEAN

SANAE
(SOUTH
AFRICA)

MAITRI
(INDIA)

SOUTHERN
OCEAN

SOUTH POLE

Scientists drill into the deep, ancient ice of Antarctica to find out about our planet's history.

SYOWA
(JAPAN)

Researchers and tourists enjoy skiing during the summer months.

Amery
Ice Shelf

ZHONGSHAN
(CHINA)

TAISHAN
(CHINA)

DAVIS
(AUSTRALIA)

South Pole

AMUNDSEN-
SCOTT (USA)

Geomagnetic
South Pole

VOSTOCK
(RUSSIA)

Weather balloons can tell scientists a lot about air temperatures, winds, and air pressure above Antarctica.

Shackleton
Ice Shelf

In the summer, the Scott Station's rugby team, the Ice Blacks, play a match against the McMurdo Station.

Ross
Ice Shelf

SCOTT
(NEW ZEALAND)

MCMURDO
(USA)

MARIO
ZUCCHELLI
(ITALY)

DUMONT
D'URVILLE
(FRANCE)

The crocodile icefish's blood contains a kind of antifreeze, so it stays liquid in the cold.

POPULATION: about 4,000 in summer and 1,000 in winter

NUMBER OF RESEARCH STATIONS: about 100 in summer and 70 in winter

WARMEST TEMPERATURE: Antarctic Peninsula (2020), 18.3°C (64.9°F)

COLDEST TEMPERATURE: east Antarctica (2010), -94.7°C (-135.8°F)

HIGHEST MOUNTAIN: Mount Vinson: 4,892 m (16,050 ft)

Key

RESEARCH STATION
ICE SHELF

45

ANTARCTIC ANIMALS

Growing up to 1.2 m (47 in) tall, emperor penguins are the largest kind of penguin. They keep warm in the extreme cold by standing close together in big groups, called huddles.

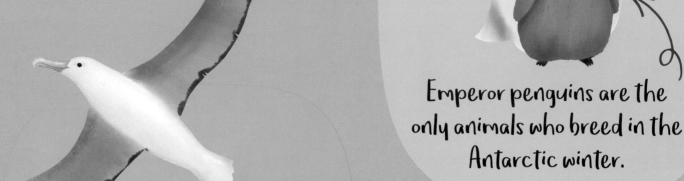

Emperor penguins are the only animals who breed in the Antarctic winter.

The wandering albatross has the largest wings of any bird—they measure 3.5 m (11.5 ft) across. It glides above the ocean in search of food, and can stay in the air for days at a time.

At 30 m (98 ft), the blue whale is the largest animal on Earth. Every summer, it travels to the waters around Antarctica to feed on tiny animals called krill.

When they are born, blue whale calves are already 8 m (26 ft) long!

ANTARCTIC NATURE AND RESEARCH

The southern lights, or aurora australis, are a display of bands of light in yellow, green, blue, red, and pink. They can be seen most clearly in Antarctica's winter sky.

The UK research station Halley VI stands on the Brunt Ice Shelf. It is made up of a row of eight pods and stands on stilts so it doesn't get buried by snow drifts.

The station's pods stand on skis, so Halley VI can easily be moved.

The mildest area of Antarctica is the Antarctic Peninsula. Here, one of the continent's few plants, the Antarctic pearlwort, blooms during the short polar summer.

Gentoo penguins and south polar skuas nest on the peninsula.